The Daddy's BOY DEVOTIONAL

A Prayer, Planning, & Activity Journal for Boys

JENNY ERLINGSSON
WITH THOR ERLINGSSON

www.milkandhoneybooks.com

Copyright © 2020 by Jenny Erlingsson, Thor Erlingsson

All rights reserved. This book is protected by copyright laws of the United States of America. This book may not be copied or reprinted for commercial gain or profit. The use of short quotations or occasional page copying for personal or group study is permitted and encouraged. Permission will be granted upon request.

Scripture quotations marked (NIV) are taken from the Holy Bible, New International Version®, NIV®. Copyright © 1973, 1978, 1984, 2011 by Biblica, Inc.™ Used by permission of Zondervan. All rights reserved worldwide. www.zondervan.com The "NIV" and "New International Version" are trademarks registered in the United States Patent and Trademark Office by Biblica, Inc.™

Scripture quotations marked (NLT) are taken from the Holy Bible, New Living Translation, copyright ©1996, 2004, 2015 by Tyndale House Foundation. Used by permission of Tyndale House Publishers, a Division of Tyndale House Ministries, Carol Stream, Illinois 60188. All rights reserved.

Scripture quotations marked (ERV) are taken from the Holy Bible: Easy-to-Read Version (ERV), International Edition© 2013, 2016 by Bible League International and used by permission. All Rights Reserved.

This book is available at:
Cover & Interior Design by Jenny Erlingsson via Canva

Reach us on the Internet: www.milkandhoneybooks.com
ISBN TP: 978-1-953000-01-9

For Worldwide Distribution, Printed in the United States of America
1 2 3 4 5 6 7 8 9 10

This Book Belongs to:

....

www.milkandhoneybooks.com

Hey!

Do you know that you were created on purpose and with a purpose? God loves you so much and when you know Jesus you are called a son of God. You are a strong and brave son of God. This journal is all about you, how much God loves you and how we can show others how much we love Him. We hope that you will use this book to draw & dream & write & read & color as you spend with Jesus. He paid a big price for you through His life and he wants you to know that you belong to Him. If you need any help, ask someone older to do this with you!

♡ **Jenny & Thor**
(Jenny's oldest son)

YOUR HEART BELONGS TO JESUS

"THE LORD IS MY STRENGTH AND MY SHIELD; MY HEART TRUSTS IN HIM, AND HE HELPS ME. MY HEART LEAPS FOR JOY, AND WITH MY SONG I PRAISE HIM."
PSALM 28:7

Week 1

In the beginning, God created everything

OUR AMAZING CREATOR

Week 1

God is an amazing creator. In the beginning of all things it is His word that set things in motion. When He spoke, light shot forth, the sun, moon and stars came into existence. But the best thing that God created wasn't the stars in the sky, the mountains or the oceans. It wasn't even the cutest puppy or the strongest elephant. The best of God's creation is you and me. God created us to watch and rule over the earth but most of all, He created us to love Him and know Him.

What are some things in creation that make you smile? Are there any plants, animals, or things in nature that remind you of God?

Write Your Thoughts

_____
_____
_____
_____
_____

| MONDAY | My Week | TUESDAY  |

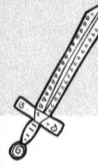 WEDNESDAY | THURSDAY

Bible Verse

FRIDAY

God created the sky and the earth. At first, the earth was completely empty. There was nothing on the earth. Darkness covered the ocean, and God's Spirit moved over the water. Then God said, "Let there be light!" And light began to shine.
Genesis 1:1-3 ERV

SATURDAY

SUNDAY

 ADAM

The one who was first
Genesis 2:4-25; 3:1-24

Adam was the first man that God created. His name means "mankind" and he was formed from the dust of the ground. God breathed his breath of life into Him. The Bible says that God took a piece of Adam and formed Eve. He made Eve as a perfect helper to Adam. This doesn't mean that she was less than or behind him. It means that she was created in the image of God too and also had the responsibility to work alongside Adam in taking care of the earth. They were both called to be friends with God. The Bible says that God walked with Adam and Eve in the cool of the day. Even when they messed up and sinned, God made a plan to fix it. He loved spending time with Adam & Eve. And He loves spending time with you. **What are ways that you can spend time with God today?**

⟵ Write Your Thoughts ⟶

_____

_____

_____

_____

_____

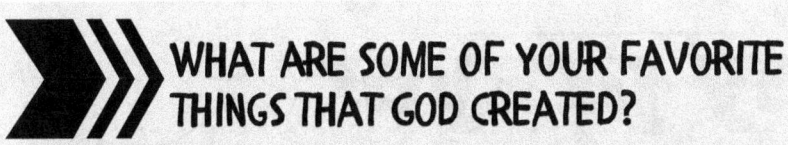

>>> WHAT ARE SOME OF YOUR FAVORITE THINGS THAT GOD CREATED?

Week 1

WHAT ELSE?

Week 1

God created the sky and the earth. At first, the earth was completely empty. There was nothing on the earth. Darkness covered the ocean, and God's Spirit moved over the water. Then God said, "Let there be light!" And light began to shine.

Genesis 1:1-3 ERV

Week 2

God Loves Me. He did a good job making me.

Week 2

I AM WONDERFULLY MADE

God has a specific plan and purpose for you and that includes how He made you. He looks at you and sees His handsome son. Sometimes when we look in the mirror we don't always feel that way. Maybe you are shorter or taller than others. Or maybe you don't walk the same or even talk the same. Sometimes we are even born with abilities that make us have to do things a little differently.

God doesn't want you to feel bad about how He made you. He wants you to see yourself the way He sees you. There are so many special gifts that he has given to just *you*. You have value because He sent Jesus to earth to remind you of how valuable and special you are. **What are some things that are special about you?**

⬅ Write Your Thoughts ➡

_____
_____
_____
_____
_____

My Week

MONDAY

TUESDAY

WEDNESDAY

THURSDAY

Bible Verse

I praise you because you made me in such a wonderful way. I know how amazing that was!

Psalm 139:14 ERV

FRIDAY

SATURDAY

SUNDAY

JOSEPH

The one who trusted God
Genesis 37-45

Are you the only child or do you have a lot of brothers and sisters? Joseph was someone who definitely knew what it was like to be in a big blended family. They were not always friendly with each and one day Joseph's own brothers sold him into slavery because they were jealous of his gifts. It was a hard time for Joseph because he went from being in the pit, to Potiphar's house as a slave, to the prison and then to the palace where the Pharoah lived. But God never stopped being with Joseph. Because Joseph trusted and obeyed God no matter what, God put him in charge of all of Egypt! He got to use his skills and gifts to help take care of the people in the land and later, his own family. God brought everyone together and helped Joseph forgive. **How can you trust God even when you are having a hard time?**

⬅ Write Your Thoughts ➡

_____

_____

_____

_____

_____

CAN YOU HELP JOSEPH GET FROM THE PIT TO THE PALACE?

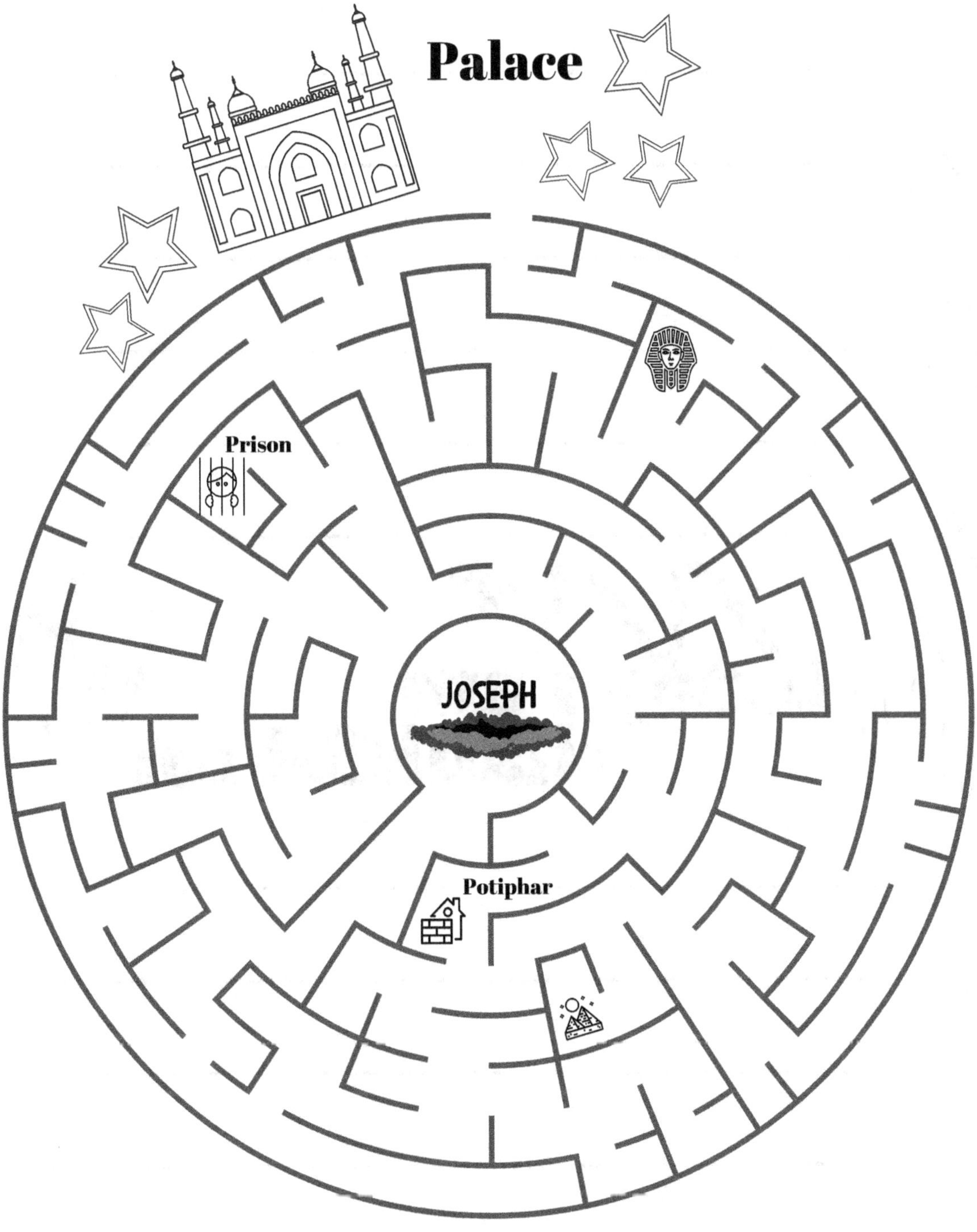

Week 2

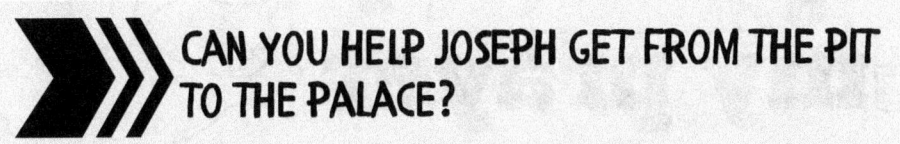

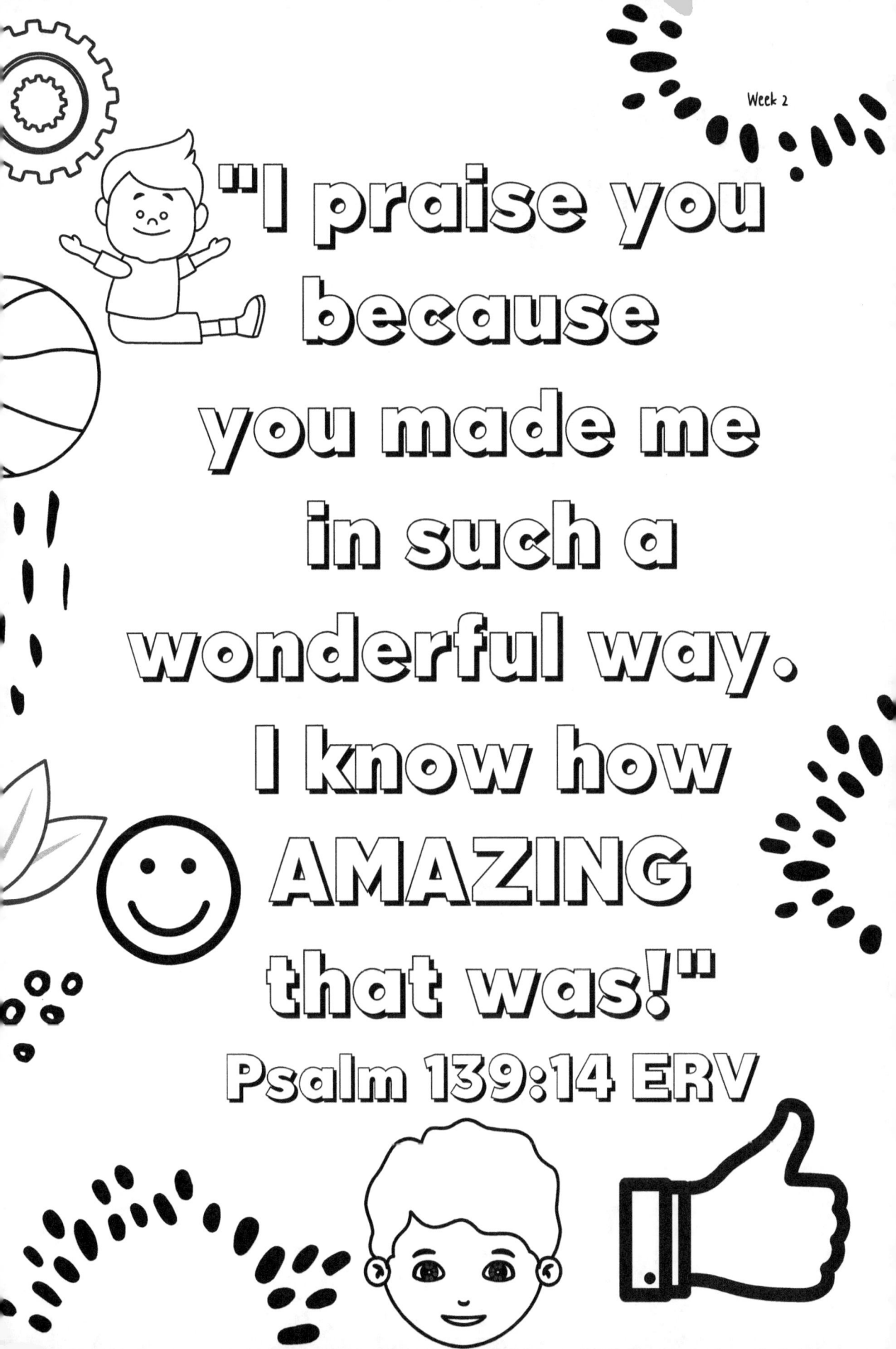

WEEK 3

When I was far away, God sent Jesus for me.

Week 3

GOD'S RESCUE PLAN

At the beginning Adam and Eve were meant to walk in deep friendship with God. But that friendship was broken when they were tempted and made the choice to sin. Sin is more than doing the wrong thing. Sin is what we do against God's commands and it keeps us from God.

But God made a plan of rescue before any of us were born. He sent his son Jesus in the form of a baby to grow up, walk with us, teach us and be with us. He came so that we would have a way back to His Father. **Have you asked Jesus to come into your life, forgive you of your sins and bring you back to God?** If not, there is no better time than now to do that. Just pray to God. Ask Jesus to forgive you of your sins and ask Him to enter your life and make you new.

⬅ Write Your Thoughts ➡

_____

_____

_____

_____

_____

_____

My Week

MONDAY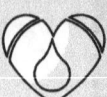

TUESDAY

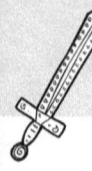
WEDNESDAY

THURSDAY

Bible Verse

Yes, God loved the world so much that he gave his only Son, so that everyone who believes in him would not be lost but have eternal life.
John 3:16 ERV

FRIDAY

SATURDAY

SUNDAY

 MOSES

The ones who was rescued & then rescued others. Exodus 2

Many years after the time of Abraham, the Israelites moved to Egypt. As a people, they became larger and stronger but Pharoah was afraid of this. He made all the Israelites slaves and then tried to kill all the baby boys. Moses was a Hebrew boy born during this sad time. But he was saved by the brave actions of his mother and sister. Moses was raised in Egypt by Pharoah's daughter but after making a huge mistake, ran away to the land of Midian. God showed himself to Moses in the most amazing way (a burning bush that didn't burn!) and told him that He would be the one to help rescue the entire nation of Israel. Just like he was rescued as a baby. Moses made the choice to obey God and because of that He became a strong leader who God trusted with more amazing things.

Is there a time that God rescued you? How can you work with Him to rescue others?

⬅ Write Your Thoughts ➡

_____

_____

_____

_____

_____

NUMBER FROM 1 TO 4 THE ACTUAL ORDER OF SOME MOMENTS IN MOSES' LIFE.

Week 3

WATER FROM A ROCK

RED SEA FALLS ON EGYPTIAN ARMY

MOSES SEES THE BURNING BUSH

MOSES TELLS THE ISRAELITES GOD WANTS TO FREE THEM

Answer: 4,3,1,2.

Week 4

Jesus paid the price that I could not pay.

Week 4

THE BEST GIFT

Have you ever wanted something so bad that cost more money than you had? It may feel impossible to get what you want. In a similar way, because of sin, people are away from God and are not able to pay the great price needed to wash away all of our sins. In the past, people used animal sacrifices to help take the place for their sins. But when Jesus came to earth He came to pay the price for our sins that we couldn't pay. Even though none of it was His fault, he put all the blame on his shoulders so that we wouldn't have to.

Jesus gave us the gift of salvation. Remember that thing you wanted? Imagine that someone gave it to you as a gift. You would be so thankful for that gift, especially because you knew you couldn't buy it for yourself. How can you show your thanks to Jesus, for the great gift that He's given to you?

⬅ **Write Your Thoughts** ➡

_____

_____

_____

_____

_____

_____

My Week

MONDAY

TUESDAY

WEDNESDAY

THURSDAY

Bible Verse

When people sin, they earn what sin pays—death. But God gives his people a free gift—eternal life in Christ Jesus our Lord.
Romans 6:23 ERV

FRIDAY

SATURDAY

SUNDAY

ZACCHAEUS
THE TAX COLLECTOR

The one who found a way
Luke 19:1-10

Zacchaeus was a man that people didn't like very much. He was a tax collector who worked with the Romans to make the Jewish people pay more taxes than they were supposed to. He did this so that he could make more money. This made people upset so he probably didn't have a lot of friends. One day Zacchaeus heard that Jesus was in town. He wanted to see Jesus but he was too short to see above the crowd. So he climbed up in a Sycamore tree to get a better look. Not only did he see Jesus but Jesus saw him! Jesus told Zacchaeus that he was going to his house to eat with him. Because of how much Jesus loved him, even when he'd done wrong things, Zacchaeus decided to change his life and give back to the people he had taken money from. **Did you know that Jesus sees you too? What is something that you can do to see Jesus a little better in your life?**

⬅ Write Your Thoughts ➡

_____

_____

_____

_____

WHAT ARE SOME OF THE GIFTS YOU CAN GIVE BACK TO JESUS IN WORSHIP

Week 4

1. _____ 
2. _____
3. _____
4. _____

TO: JESUS
FROM:

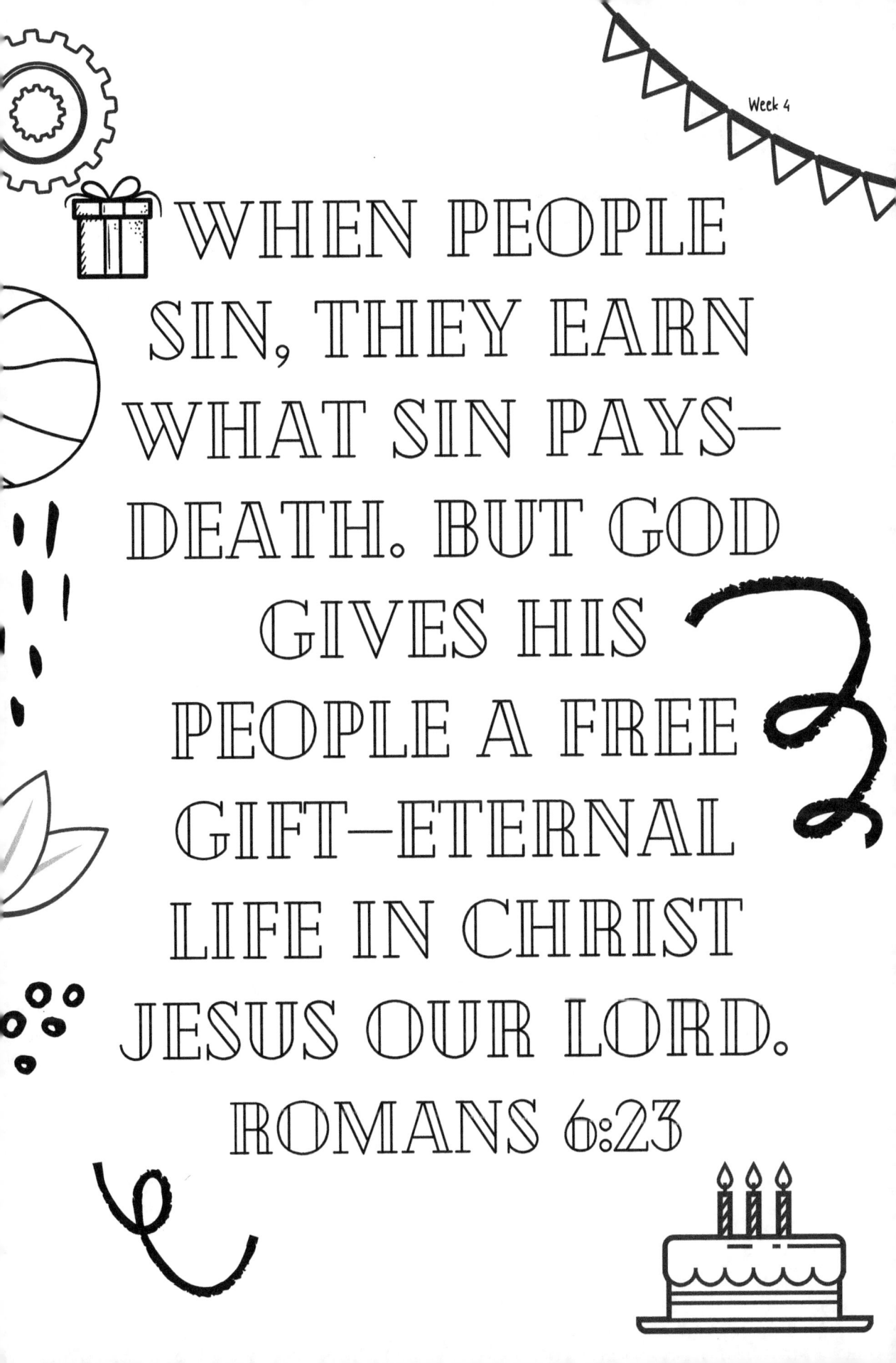

Week 5

I am made brand new & promised life in heaven that will never end.

Week 5

BRAND NEW

After Jesus gave us the gift of salvation by dying on the cross, He came back to life after three days. Through His resurrection we have new, eternal life. When we know Jesus, we are not the same person we were before Jesus. All the dirty sin has been washed away and we are a new creation.

God comes into our lives and creates our hearts brand new, just like He did at creation. Because of this new life we can live in new ways. We can pray to God and talk with Him. We can say no to the things that are not like God.

What is exciting to you about being a new creation in Jesus?

Write Your Thoughts

_____
_____
_____
_____
_____
_____

My Week

MONDAY

TUESDAY

WEDNESDAY

THURSDAY

Bible Verse

Therefore, if anyone is in Christ, the new creation has come: The old has gone, the new is here!
2 Corinthians 5:17 ERV

FRIDAY

SATURDAY

SUNDAY

THE MAN IN THE GRAVEYARD

The one Jesus set free
Mark 5:1-20

Jesus came into the world to destroy all the evil things the devil has done to creation and to people. There was a man who suffered for a long time. Jesus and his disciples found him after they crossed over a stormy sea.

This man had so many evil spirits in him that he could not be with people. He lived around graveyards and was all alone. But Jesus saw him and loved him and met him so that this man could be set free. Jesus threw the demons out of him and told him to tell everyone he knew about what God had done. Jesus doesn't want any of us to live in fear or to keep anything else that would put chains on us.

What is something Jesus wants to free you from and make new in your life?

◄ Write Your Thoughts ►

_____

_____

_____

_____

▶▶▶ DRAW A LINE TO MATCH EACH MAN TO HIS MISSION

Week 5

1 MOSES
(BOOK OF EXODUS)

WALLS OF JERICHO

2 JOSEPH
(BOOK OF GENESIS)

MOUNTAIN OF GOD

3 JOSHUA
(BOOK OF JOSHUA)

LETTERS TO CHURCHES

4 DAVID
(BOOK OF 1 SAMUEL)

LEADING EYGPT

5 PAUL
(BOOK OF ROMANS & MORE)

KING OF ISRAEL

ANSWERS: 1-MOUNTAIN, 2-EGYPT, 3-WALLS, 4-CROWN, 5-SCROLL

Week 6

I am a son of God. I can be close to Him.

Week 6

CLOSE TO GOD

When we know Jesus, we are invited to be close to Father God. Everything that kept us from God is no more. And you know what is so beautiful about this friendship? We are brought into the family of God and you are called a son of God. Just like in the first garden when Adam and Eve were a son and daughter of God. This is such a sweet name that God gives us because it means that no matter what is happening in our lives, we belong to Him. Even if you have no parents, or one parent or live with your grandparents or someone else who takes care of you, you can always know that you have a place with God because He calls you His son. And that means you can always run to Him for whatever you need. **Is there something even now that you want to ask your Father in heaven for?**

⬅ Write Your Thoughts ➡

_____

_____

_____

_____

_____

_____

My Week

MONDAY

TUESDAY

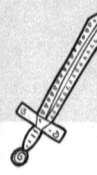

WEDNESDAY

THURSDAY

Bible Verse

With Jesus as our high priest, we can feel free to come before God's throne where there is grace. There we receive mercy and kindness to help us when we need it.
Hebrews 4:16 ERV

FRIDAY

SATURDAY

SUNDAY

THE BLIND MAN

The one who was healed
Genesis 37-45

There was a man that had been blind his whole life. He sat on the side of the road begging for money and food. We don't know all of his story but we know that he was alone and didn't have any family near him. Jesus saw him and healed him by putting mud in his eyes. Doesn't it remind you of God forming Adam out of the dirt and mud? He told the blind man to go wash his eyes off in a special pool and when he did, he could see! But when the man showed himself to the leaders in his synagogue they were angry because they didn't like Jesus and told the man he could never come back. Jesus heard what happened and took the time to go and find the man. He wanted him to know that not only was he healed, he was loved and that the man always had a family with Jesus.

What helps you remember that you belong to God?

◄ Write Your Thoughts ►

_____

_____

_____

_____

_____

WHAT DO YOU SEE?

Week 6

CAN YOU FIND THE...
pancakes, tacos, hamburger, watermelon, doughnut, blender & apple?

Week 6

With Jesus as our high priest, we can feel free to come before God's throne where there is grace. There we receive mercy and kindness to help us when we need it.

Hebrews 4:16 ERV

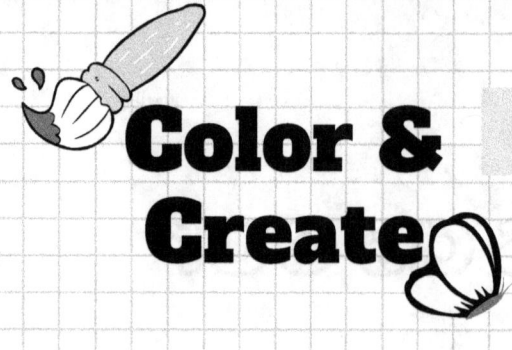

Week 7

Everything Jesus has, He wants to give me too.

A Royal Prince

Week 7

Knowing Jesus means being born again into God's Kingdom. That makes you a prince in his kingdom. A prince knows that he is loved and cared for. Think about the prince and princesses you read about in stories or even see from different countries. They know that they are very important to the countries they serve. They are treasured and their daddy has everything that they need.

Being a prince in God's kingdom means the same thing and even more. Jesus has all the power and rules over everything . When we know Jesus we can ask for everything He has for us. God wants us to dream big and to dream with Him to see the world changed all around us. **What is something in your life that you want to see God change?**

⬅ Write Your Thoughts ➡

_____
_____
_____
_____
_____
_____

My Week

MONDAY

TUESDAY

 WEDNESDAY

THURSDAY

Bible Verse

> We know who he is, and we know who we are: Father and children. And we know we are going to get what's coming to us—an unbelievable inheritance! We go through exactly what Christ goes through. If we go through the hard times with him, then we're certainly going to go through the good times with him!
> Romans 8:17 MSG

FRIDAY

SATURDAY

SUNDAY

 ABRAHAM

The one who followed God's call to GO
Genesis 12

God had big plans for Abraham that would involve not just his family, but all of us! Abraham followed the call of God to go to a new place. God was choosing Abraham to be the start of something new. During that time in history, many people worshiped false gods. They made fake gods out of wood and metal and stone and bowed down before them. But God chose Abraham to be the father to a new nation, a people that would follow the one true God, the God of Adam and Noah. When Abraham said yes, he didn't understand how it would all happen, especially since he didn't have any children yet, but he trusted God. He was even called God's friend. Abraham knew that God would provide everything he needed. Even a son.

Is there a big decision God wants you to follow Him in?
Maybe its something new He wants to bring into you life.

⬅ Write Your Thoughts ➡

_____

_____

_____

_____

_____

COLOR IN ABRAHAM'S JOURNEY AND THEN DRAW YOUR OWN JOURNEY BELOW

Week 7

ABRAHAM

ME

Week 8

Jesus sent the Holy Spirit to live in me and help me.

Week 8

OUR SPECIAL HELPER

Before Jesus went back to Heaven He told the disciples that He would send them a comforter, a special helper that would give them power to be more like Jesus. The Holy Spirit lives inside of us. We don't ever have to feel lonely or be afraid because He reminds us of God's love for us and the gift of salvation Jesus gave us.

Sometimes it's hard to understand how this happens but think about yourself. You are a whole person that is made up of many layers. You are **1.)** body **2.)** soul (mind, thoughts & feelings) and **3.)** heart (spirit). So when we believe in Jesus, God the Son, we get to be close to God the Father and be the house for God, the Holy Spirit. **What do you need the Holy Spirit to help you with today?**

⟵ Write Your Thoughts ⟶

_____
_____
_____
_____
_____

MONDAY  My Week TUESDAY

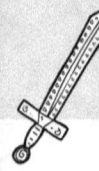 WEDNESDAY THURSDAY

Bible Verse

> Since you are now God's children, he has sent the Spirit of his Son into your hearts. The Spirit cries out, "Abba, Father."
> Galatians 4:6 ERV

FRIDAY

SATURDAY

SUNDAY

 # PHILLIP

The one who did great things for God
Acts 8:26-40

Phillip was a man that God used to do amazing things! He didn't start off on a stage or with an important title, at least in the eyes of others. He became a leader because he helped serve people. He brought food to those who needed it and did the jobs that others didn't always want to do. He did those things well and was faithful with the gifts God gave him. The Bible tells us that he shared the good news with a man from another country and as soon as that man was baptized, the Holy Spirit took Phillip away to another place in an instant! Can you imagine zooming through time and space to get to somewhere else super quick? Phillip saw people healed and later, when he had daughters, the Bible says that they all prophesied and spoke the words of God. It doesn't matter how big or small, God wants you to do everything for Him. **What is something big you can do for God, even if no one sees it?**

⬅ Write Your Thoughts ➡

_____

_____

_____

_____

_____

WHAT ARE SOME WAYS THAT YOU DO OR CAN HELP OTHER PEOPLE?

Week 8

Week 8

"SINCE YOU ARE NOW GOD'S CHILDREN, HE HAS SENT THE SPIRIT OF HIS SON INTO YOUR HEARTS. THE SPIRIT CRIES OUT, "ABBA, FATHER.""
GALATIANS 4:6 ERV

WEEK 9

Holy Spirit helps me live a life that makes Him smile.

Week 9

LISTENING TO GOD

Living our lives for Jesus is the best choice we can make but it's not always easy. There are so many things that may take our attention away from God. This is why Jesus wants us to have the Holy Spirit as a helper. The Holy Spirit begins to lead us through the Bible, when we pray, when we worship and especially when we lean close and listen to Him. Many times He speaks to us in a still small voice that we hear in our hearts because He wants us to get quiet and focused enough to listen. Even when we feel like God is telling us no, we can trust that its because He loves us and has a better plan for us. When we turn off the television or games or take time away from playing to spend time with Him, we get filled with all that we need to live a life that makes God smile. **What do you need to do (or turn off) to help you listen to God better?**

Write Your Thoughts

_____

_____

_____

_____

_____

_____

My Week

MONDAY

TUESDAY

 ### WEDNESDAY

THURSDAY

Bible Verse

>
> So I tell you, live the way the Spirit leads you. Then you will not do the evil things your sinful self wants.
> Galatians 5:16 ERV

FRIDAY

SATURDAY

SUNDAY

DAVID

The one who became king
1 Samuel 16

David was called a man after God's own heart. That means that no matter what he did, he always went back to wanting to please God. He was chosen to be the next King of Israel at an early age because God saw his heart and how special he was, even when others didn't. He was the one who killed the enemy giant Goliath and also the one who brought peace to King Saul through his worship. Even when David made some big mistakes later on in his life, he didn't wait long to ask for forgiveness and did whatever He could to make himself right with God again. God loves when we stay close to him even when we do the wrong thing, because he is the only one who can make us right again through Jesus.

Is there a choice you've made that you know didn't please God, that you need to make right?

⬅ Write Your Thoughts ➡

_____
_____
_____
_____
_____

FIND THE WORDS THAT DESCRIBE KING DAVID'S LIFE

Week 9

```
D A V I D O J S P
W G W O W G K T S
L I O I L F I O Q
H H R L J Z N N S
A E S L I N G E H
R A H W O A T S E
M R I B A T T L E
O T P T X L Z H P
R C R O W N P M Z
```

Word List

GOLIATH
WORSHIP
STONES
BATTLE
DAVID
CROWN

SLING
ARMOR
SHEEP
HEART
KING
OIL

Week 9

So I tell you, live the way the Spirit leads you. Then you will not do the evil things your sinful self wants.

Galatians 5:16 ERV

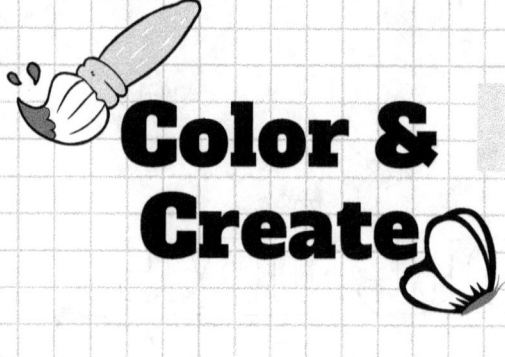

Week 10

My God is so strong and He is so Good.

Week 10

WE TRUST HIM

Many times we see so many hard things happen around us and we may not feel like we are strong or powerful enough to do something. This is why its so important to remember that you are a son of God because of what Jesus did for you on the cross. Even though we may not be the strongest or the smartest or richest or even bravest, our Father God is.
He is the strongest, bravest, smartest, richest and He will take care of all the things that we give to him. He cares abut what we care about, from the smallest to the biggest thing. Not only that, but he also loves being with you and having fun with you. We can trust that we are safe and protected by Him and this should bring us all kinds of joy.

What is something fun you can do with God today?

⟵ Write Your Thoughts ⟶

_____
_____
_____
_____
_____
_____

MONDAY	My Week	TUESDAY 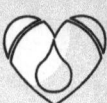

 WEDNESDAY | THURSDAY

Bible Verse

The Lord your God is with you. He is like a powerful soldier. He will save you. He will show how much he loves you and how happy he is with you. He will laugh and be happy about you,
Zephaniah 3:17 ERV

FRIDAY

SATURDAY

SUNDAY

 CALEB

The one who believed in God's strength
Numbers 13

Caleb was a brave man who believed that God could do anything! When Moses sent twelve men out to look through the promised land that God was giving them, they saw lots of great things but they were also scared of the people of the land. Caleb and Joshua were a part of this team but they were the *only ones* who were not afraid. They believed that God had given them the land and that they could win any battle they faced. Because Caleb and Joshua trusted in God, they were able to enter the promised land when the others their age could not. And even as an old man, Caleb was not afraid to fight for God in his new home.

Name two ways you can be brave like Caleb and trust in God's power today?

◁ Write Your Thoughts ▷

_____

_____

_____

_____

_____

>>> CALEB WAS FROM THE TRIBE OF JUDAH, REPRESENTED BY THE LION.

Week 10

WHO ELSE COMES FROM THE ISRAELI TRIBE OF JUDAH?

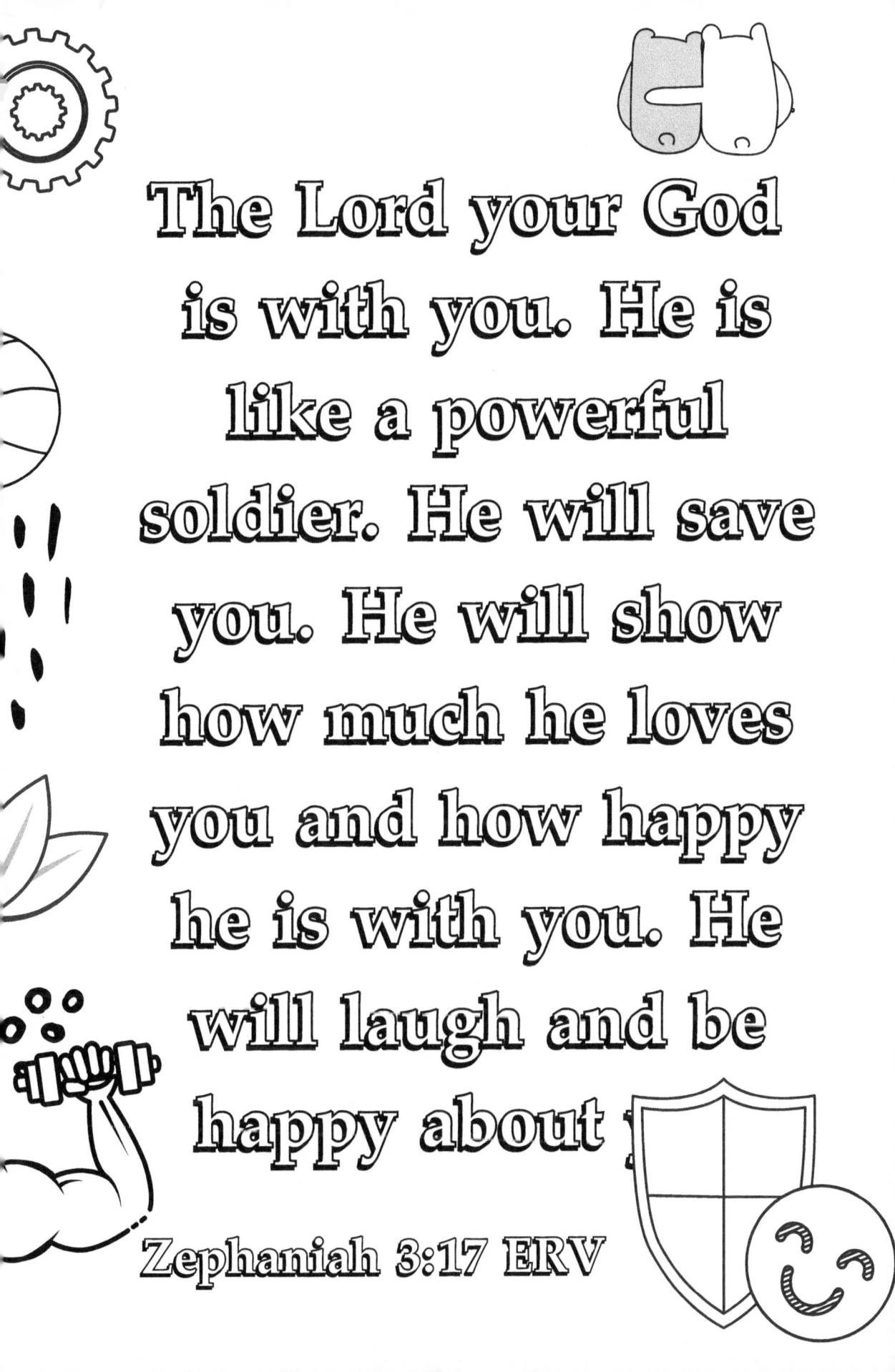

Week 11

Jesus can do amazing things in my life and in the lives of others.

Week 11

NOTHING IS IMPOSSIBLE

The Bible is full of so many stories where God did amazing things in the lives of the people who knew Him. He brought healing, increased food, set people free from demons and even raised some from the dead. And isn't it cool that God never changes? That means the things He did back then, He can do and does now. The name of Jesus is more powerful than any other name around and when we speak His name and believe in Him, everything else can't stand up against Him. There may be things going on in your life that seem dark or fearful or painful. But never forget that nothing is impossible with God and that even your faith in Jesus can accomplish great things.

Right now, speak the name of Jesus as you pray for your family and friends.

⬅ Write Your Thoughts ➡

_____

_____

_____

_____

_____

_____

My Week

MONDAY

TUESDAY

 WEDNESDAY

THURSDAY

Bible Verse

➤➤➤→

God can do anything!
Luke 1:37 ERV

FRIDAY

SATURDAY

SUNDAY

JOSHUA

The one who was courageous
Joshua 6:1-27

Joshua was the assistant to Moses, the leader of Israel. He helped Moses and learned how to lead people from Moses' example. He was a brave man who wasn't afraid of any enemy but believed that God would always win. But the best part about Joshua wasn't his bravery but in how he wanted to know God more. He wanted to be with God. Even after Moses left his prayers times with God, Joshua stayed longer. It's because of this strong faith that God placed Joshua over the people of Israel. God knew that his faith would help the people obey and win every battle. Because of how Joshua listened to God, Israel's first battle in the promised land was won and a whole city came tumbling down.

Is there something that you are facing that needs courageous faith?

⬅ Write Your Thoughts ➡

_____
_____
_____
_____
_____

Week 12

I want my life and my words to spread the good news about Jesus.

Week 12

SHARING THE GOOD NEWS

One of the last things Jesus said to his followers before He left the earth was to go and make more followers out of all the nations on earth. Knowing Jesus is good news and He wants us to share that news with everyone around this. We don't just do this with the words we say, we also tell the good news with the way we act, the way we love and care for others. We share the good news when we help others and show kindness. Even when we don't know what to do, the Holy Spirit in us helps us reflect the light of Jesus to the world around us. When we follow Jesus, and obey Him through our words and our lives, we point the way for others to know Him too. Everyone around is invited to go to Jesus, be forgiven of their sins and have new life in Him.

Who in your life needs good news today?

⬅ Write Your Thoughts ➡

_____

_____

_____

_____

_____

_____

MONDAY 	My Week	TUESDAY

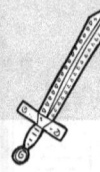 WEDNESDAY | THURSDAY

Bible Verse

FRIDAY

> So go and make followers of all people in the world. Baptize them in the name of the Father and the Son and the Holy Spirit.
> Matthew 28:19 ERV

SATURDAY

SUNDAY

 PAUL

The one who spread the news
Acts 9

Saul was a man that did not like followers of Jesus and worked very hard to see them destroyed. He was on the scene when the first man was killed for believing in Jesus. But Jesus had a special plan for Saul. He met him on the road in all His power and glory and told Saul who He was, the one that Saul was fighting. Jesus told Saul that he was going to use him to share the good news not just to other Jewish people, but to people in other countries. To make the change clear, Jesus changed Saul's name to Paul. Because of Paul, we have many books in the Bible that show us how to live a life that pleases God. And many places around the world received the good news because of Paul's dedication to tell the truth about who Jesus is. **Why is the news about Jesus so good? What does it mean for us?**

⬅ Write Your Thoughts ➡

_____

_____

_____

_____

_____

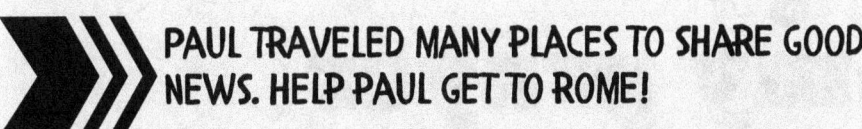

PAUL TRAVELED MANY PLACES TO SHARE GOOD NEWS. HELP PAUL GET TO ROME!

Week 12

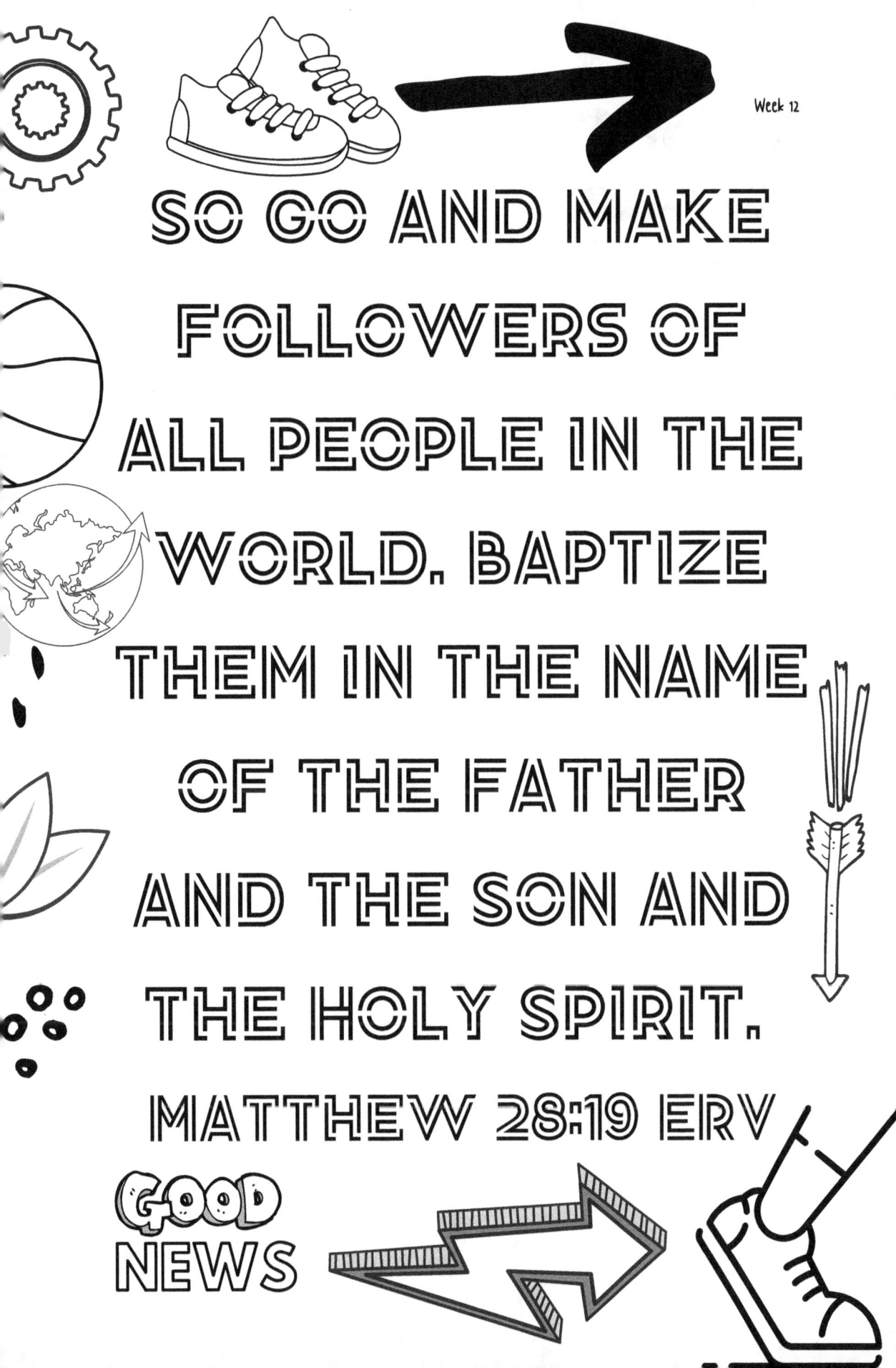

MORE RESOURCES!

BOOKS

- Milk & Honey in the Land of Fire & Ice
- Becoming His: Finding Your Place as a Daughter of God

JOURNALS & PLANNERS

- The Daddy's Boy Devotional
- Milk & Honey Women Study & Prayer Journal
- The Cultivational Planner: A Devotional Planner for Women
- Dwell: Bible Study & Prayer Journal
- Milk & Honey Women Devotional Journal

WE ARE ALWAYS COMING OUT WITH NEW RESOURCES, INCLUDING MORE FOR KIDS! SIGN UP AT WWW.MILKANDHONEYBOOKS.COM FOR INFO AND FREEBIES!

About the Author/Designer

Jenny Erlingsson is wife to her amazing viking husband and mother to four cute and fierce mocha drops. After over twelve years of serving in pastoral ministry in Alabama, she and her family currently live in Iceland working in various areas of ministry. Jenny is passionate about empowering others, especially women through her writing and speaking. She is also the author of **Milk & Honey in the Land of Fire & Ice** and **Becoming His: Finding Your Place as a Daughter of God**

MORE AT WWW.MILKANDHONEYBOOKS.COM